D1452649

The Smoke Week
September 11-21, 2001

Ellis Avery

Arlington, Virginia

Published by Gival Press, an imprint of Gival Press, LLC.
For information please write:
Gival Press, LLC, P. O. Box 3812,
Arlington, Virginia 22203.
Website: givalpress.com

First Edition

ISBN 1-928589-24-3

Library of Congress Card Number 2003109728
Photo of Ellis Avery by Sharon Marcus.
Format and design by Ken Schellenberg.

Excerpts from *The Smoke Week* appear in slightly different form in:

Ohioana Quarterly, Vol. XLV, No. 3, Fall 2002.
Published by the Ohioana Library Association.
Eleven, an artist book/CD project published by Booklyn, 2002. Book artists: Marshall Weber with Christopher Wilde, Sarah Parkel, Alison Williams. CD recording produced by Revolucien Wreckidz.

For the dead, over here and over there.

And for Sharon, with love.

Contents

September 8

Emergency

The Saturday after Labor Day, at the last party wrung from the summer, my friend Kathy showed us a picture of her brother's two boys. *That's Christopher,* she said. *The six-year-old. You've got to hear this. Last winter my brother told me that Christopher came home from school upset because*—she adopted a child's serious mien—*some of the kids in music class had been acting up and the teacher made them all stand by the wall, even kids like him who'd been quiet.*

My brother—Kathy's voice turned parental—*said that Christopher should tell the music teacher that he knew it was important to keep the class in order, but his feelings were hurt and he wanted an apology. But the next day the teacher wasn't in school, and then the day after that they had off for snow.*

Christopher seemed happy enough to stay home from school on Friday, but then, late Saturday morning, there was a knock at the door. 'It's the police,' said a voice. 'Open up.'

My brother got up from lounging in front of the TV, and my sister-in-law came down from giving my other nephew a bath. So there they were at the door, him in his boxer shorts and her in a ratty bathrobe with a naked baby on her hip.

'We had a call about a child,' said the cop, looking them over.

And then Christopher came padding eagerly down the stairs. 'Are the police here?'

'What? Did you call them?' asked my brother.

Kathy took on the face of an aggrieved six-year-old and said, *'Music teacher… stand by the wall… hurt my feelings… apologize…couldn't tell her Thursday…couldn't tell her Friday… emergency…call 911!'*

Once the cop decided that my brother and his wife weren't actually beating their children, he tried to explain to Christopher when and when not to call for help. 'So, okay, what if the house were on fire?'

'I would call 911.'

'That's right, good. Now what if your feelings were hurt?'

'I would call 911.'

The cop looked at my brother and said, 'You gotta work with him on this one.'

January 17, 1983

Diary

I saw a show about Nostradamus. He lived about 400 years ago and predicted many things. For the future he predicts a great famine in 1986 (I'll be 14) and earthquakes in 1988.

There's more. He predicts a great war coming from the Middle East in 1994, and the destruction of one of the Great New Cities. 27 years of war, then 1000 years of peace. The world will end around 3700. Meanwhile I'm moving to Canada. After watching that show I have a stomache.

September 8, 9, 10, 11

Ordinary Time

The last weekend. Jennifer's birthday, Central Park. Pear tatin. Champagne. The smoked fish from Russ & Daughters lay on its sheet of waxed paper like a ritual offering: the sacrament of the picnic. A doctor. An architect. A pair of ringletted cherub children. Kathy told stories about her family.

The sun set. The moths rose. We went to the doctor's apartment to watch the US Open women's finals: magnificent Venus, magnificent Serena.

In the morning, Sharon and I made love and then read, tangled together. I hurried through *Woman: an Intimate Geography* and met the book group girls that night—Sara, Katrin, Kathy, Asya, Melissa, and Lee. Cassy couldn't make it; she and Julian were practicing for their INS interview the next morning. We talked about mating monkeys over cupcakes Kathy had frosted to look like breasts.

On Monday I worked on a book review for a magazine. I set aside Tuesday morning for copying my novel and sending it out.

Sharon left to go work in Princeton at six on Tuesday morning. I couldn't fall back asleep, so I made some breakfast. I was surprised by soft shadows of trees on the buildings across the street. I live in the East Village, in Manhattan: my windows face south, so the morning play of light is early come, quickly gone. I usually miss it. I reminded myself to vote and dropped my manuscript off at the Astor Place Kinko's. *Come back in an hour*, they said, so I went next door to the K-Mart. I bought a toothbrush and soap, some toilet paper. I later looked at my receipt: it said nine AM.

September 11

At First Sight

I walked out of the K-Mart and saw the sky, a perfect September blue. And crossing it, a black cloud of smoke, roiling right to left over Lafayette Street.

The city couldn't have decided to burn poor Kate Millet out of her apartment on the Bowery, because the cloud was blowing the wrong way, but something very near was on fire, judging from the amount of smoke. *It's at Broadway and Houston,* I guessed, a block over and eight down. Was the Angelika Theater burning?

I looked around for an explanation. No one else was even looking up. Then a man walked quickly by, talking into his cell phone. *A plane just crashed into the World Trade Center,* he said.

But that's thirty blocks away. What a sick joke, I thought, but I trotted after him and tugged his sleeve. *Is it true?* I asked.

Yeah, he said, and kept moving.

I had my copies to pick up, so I bought a hot chocolate and stayed where I was, under the black cube sculpture on Astor Place. Would anyone else notice the smoke?

Most didn't. The early light fell on hundreds of faces, as people thronged toward Broadway or poured down stairs to get on subways. Men pushed brooms or carried briefcases, girls hiked up their school uniforms. Campaigners dressed in their Election Day best passed out flyers for the mayoral primary. Guys in a van honked at guys in a car. Women jogged, adding those funny running-in-place steps at the crosswalks. And one college student, a throwback to 1999, pushed, pushed, pushed down Lafayette on her little silver scooter, sundress fluttering, her face in the sun like hot new glass. Astor Place was like an Edward Hopper painting, its anomalous broad bright spaces teeming on this perfectly blue September day. A few people, mostly with cell phones, stared up at the blossoming horror, a few pointed.

And one woman ran, throbbing down the block, her nice work scarf surging from side to side. I could see the whites of her eyes from across the street.

Of course I had to pick up my copies. I was like the others: hostage to my so-called future. We were still swaddled in the old world, and she had burst through to the new.

September 11

See, Saw

I walked into Kinko's and heard somebody mumble, *Fucking terrorists.*

That was quick, I thought. *How does he know it wasn't an accident?*

I tried to pay for my copies with a credit card, but the woman said, *All our phone lines are down due to what just happened.* She produced a form I didn't know existed: I filled it out and she told me she'd run the charge later. *A man was just in here*, she said. *He was late for a meeting at the World Trade Center; he was shaking.* She looked outside. *I hope it ain't as bad as it looks.*

The enormity of the morning first struck me as logistical: where could I stand so I could see? How far? How high? *I live in the East Village: my windows face south. I saw the soft shadows of trees on the buildings across the street.* I forgot, and then remembered, that I see, saw, the World Trade Center out my window every day.

I climbed four flights, set down my things, and walked into the front room.

September 11

What I Saw out the Window

Both buildings were on fire. Could the plane have ricocheted between them?

I had never noticed how their windows looked like scales. Both buildings looked like fish eaten up by fire. Like Jennifer's smoked fish on its sheet of waxed paper, on fire.

Like two lungs, on fire.

Like two beehives: healthy cells below, damaged cells above, an orange layer of flame marking the division between whole and blasted.

Then smoke covered the south tower and it was gone.

Summer 1996

Once Upon a Time

I moved here five years ago with two friends, Jan and Janna. In love with our new lives, we took the subway up to the Cloisters and down to Battery Park. We took the dangling tram across the river to Roosevelt Island, we kayaked the Hudson, we walked the Brooklyn Bridge.

We took the elevator to the top of the World Trade Center one night. There was a place you could look out the window for free. The world we saw was black and blue and gold, wedges and columns of bright window and dark steel. Small but visible night-shift men and women worked at their desks, framed and lit like Byzantine saints.

The buildings blazed upward, lit the sky and one another, aloft. Far below, we saw tiny streets, the very names of which—in a gridded city of numbered blocks and avenues—seemed dim, threadlike, Dickensian: *Old Slip, Coenties Slip, Thames, Vesey, Gouverneur, Maiden Lane.* From above, at night, they formed a dark filigree, a patina in which the luminous towers burned all the brighter.

The whole thing made us limp with pleasure. When we had our fill, we took the elevator down, looking up at the mirrored ceiling and twirling in circles, arms out. And each of us in her own way said this prayer to the city we had seen: *Ravish my heart. Take me with you.*

September 11
It's No Accident

After I saw the south tower go, I turned on the radio and Sharon called. *I called before. Did you get my message?*

I didn't listen to my messages; the World Trade Center was on fire.

They hit the Pentagon too.

What, is there a pentagon-shaped garden downtown?

No, the Pentagon Pentagon.

Oh my god. There were two planes?

No, there were three planes. One plane flew into each tower and one plane flew into the Pentagon.

My heart beat fast and my hands went cold and tingly.

Even if the city doesn't burn, I said, *they might turn off the electricity and the water. I should get food. Call me back in forty-five minutes?*

I'll try, but I keep getting busy signals.

I picked up the phone again to call my mother, but I couldn't get through.

September 11
Ourselves, Only More So

Sharon? I said, when the phone rang again.

It's Akiko. Are you okay? Is Sharon? Your friends?

Yes, yes, so far. You? Your husband?

Yes, yes. We say this is kowai, she said. *It's scary.*

Oh, kawaii is cute, but kowai is scary.

Yes, totally different meaning. I would still like to come to your house tomorrow, but maybe.

Maybe it's a little difficult. Maybe some other time.

Yes, I would like that. She paused. *Do you think I should go to class today?*

Maybe it's better to stay home, I said.

Okay. Kiotsukete, she said, *take care.*

Be safe, Akiko-san, I said.

Akiko and I studied Japanese tea ceremony together, and helped each other practice English and Japanese. I was flattered that she thought I would know what to do.

I thought about her alone on the ninth floor of her high-rise apartment. If her building caught fire, she could be trapped. If the electricity went out, she would have to climb all those stairs. If she were a refugee from her apartment, it would be terrifying to be alone with good-but-not-great English, looking for her husband. I thought of tea class, that low-slung building, that deep stone basement, the utter calm of the teachers, the presence of other Japanese speakers. On the third try, I was able to call out. *Maybe you should go to class after all*, I said, *Maybe it's safer. Can you call your husband and give him the number there?*

Okay, she said. *Thank you for calling.*

Kiotsukete, I said.

Be safe, she said.

September 11

Two Seconds

After Akiko called, I went out to get food. When I left, the north tower was standing, a body with a sawn-open chest and flaming heart. I heard the sirens screaming down Second Avenue and still trusted that the firefighters could save it.

I bought a gallon of water, a liter of seltzer, frozen shrimp dumplings (should the stove and fridge still work), a bag of baby carrots, three yogurts, two vegetable juices, one orange juice, and a box of crackers. And, because they might be my last, I bought treats: a tub of cashew butter, a Toblerone, fresh figs. I found a box of candles for sale and I got that too.

As I filled my baskets, I saw a very small child systematically touching every candy bar while a woman's urgent voice called *Lucy! Lucy!* The woman finally apprehended her child with a quick shake. *I turn my back for* two seconds *and what happens?*

Like a bug-eyed Yuppie survivalist, I stood with my heavy baskets behind a man placidly buying a single bag of chips, behind Lucy and her mother buying a juice box and salad greens. I felt like that lone running woman on Astor Place.

When I walked outside twenty people were crowded on the sidewalk around a television and someone was filming them.

And when I went home a man looked me in the eye without a leer. *Isn't this awful?* his face said. I felt singed by his compassion.

And when I got to the top of the stairs and looked out the window, the north tower was gone.

September 11

Contingency

Black smoke filled the sky. It coiled in distinct shapes, thick and bulbous, blooming like brains. I turned on the radio and Sharon called again. Another hijacked plane had crashed outside Pittsburgh. It had taken her half an hour to get through.

On the radio they're saying, if you're below Canal Street, walk north. If they start saying to walk if you're below Houston Street, I'm leaving, I said. *These rat-trap tenements would go up like tissue paper. I'll go to Central Park and get in the lake in case everything burns. I've packed my computer disk in a zip-lock bag and I'm looking for something to tie my glasses to my face. This must sound so stupid. Okay, if the fire sweeps north, I can go to tea ceremony and hide in the basement. If another plane crashes into the Empire State Building, the fire could come from north and south. The city would collapse: all the firefighters would be downtown; there'd be no one to send. So I could go to the water. There were those two thick pieces of Styrofoam I saw under the stairs. I could tape them together and boogie-board across the East River to Brooklyn. Should I go get them?*

Yes.

Don't hang up. I'll be right back. Hi.

Hi. Did you tape them together?

Not yet.

Do it now. Do we have anything waterproof?

There's duct tape, I said. *Oh, this is crazy.*

We sat quietly on the phone, listening to the radio and the sirens. One of us said, *It is unbearable to be apart from you right now.*

Sharon was at her office in Princeton and Manhattan was sealed, except to ferries and pedestrians leaving by bridge. No subways were running, no New Jersey Transit trains either.

I could walk across one of the downtown bridges to Brooklyn and try to find a cab willing to take me through Brooklyn, into Staten Island, and cross the Bayonne Bridge to New Jersey. And then what?

I could walk a hundred and seventy three blocks and cross the George Washington Bridge to New Jersey. And then what?

Or I could take one of the ferries and cross the Hudson to New Jersey. And then what?

Yeah, Newark Airport to Princeton is $90 by cab. If you can find one.

Our plan: if they let trains in, Sharon would come home. If they let trains out but not in, I would go to her. If Manhattan remained sealed, she would stay in New Jersey and I would stay wherever seemed safest here. We made a list of places in Princeton she might stay, numbers I could contact, in order, if we couldn't find each other. It started with Liz, my favorite high school English teacher, and ended with the Novotel Hotel on Route 1.

Call my mother, I said. *And call Loudi in Brooklyn to say where you're staying. I can get a call out to Brooklyn but not to you.*

I called what friends I could. The cordless phone cut out; I used a rotary phone I'd once bought as a stage prop. My friend Loudi called with word from Sharon: she'd been able to leave a message for my mother, and she'd reached Liz: of course Sharon could stay over, we both could. Now all I could do was wait by the radio as smoke poured upward, until they said I could join her, until the trains ran out again.

September 11
What Happened?

Nineteen men armed with box-cutting knives had attacked the military and economic centers of my country. The tallest buildings in my city, each 110 stories high, had collapsed in on themselves, their steel frames melting from the two thousand degree heat of twenty-four thousand gallons of burning airplane fuel. The biggest building in the world (after the factory that made the hijacked planes), home to the biggest war machine ever known, lay ruptured and smoking. There was a wrecked plane in a Pennsylvania field. Where had it been pointed?

It required so little. Just a fingertip to nudge our big planes toward our big buildings. Just a plane ticket and an Exacto knife. The enemy paid for the rest.

Did amputees, in the age before anesthetic, find it in themselves to admire the clean lines of the doctor's saw? I heard animal noises seeping from my mouth as I watched the black smoke rise.

September 11

I Still Haven't Mentioned

The obvious:

People died.

Panic is this selfish.

I waited by the radio. I heard about a man who had walked all the way home to Ninety-second Street, his face smeared with ash, his suit soaked through with sweat.

I heard about a man who fled his home after a computer blew in through the window.

I heard about an old couple tottering across the Williamsburg Bridge. They said nobody would hurt them in Brooklyn.

And then I heard about a firefighter, killed by a falling body.

I covered my face with my hands. The smoke coiled upward, constantly giving birth to itself. There was a hideous solidity to it; it was our new buildings. And then the trains were running again, off the island but not on.

September 11

Lucky

The street outside was eerie, car-less, full of silent people walking south in slow twos and threes. The restaurants were open, filled with worried people sitting alone, talking on cell phones, or worried people sitting together, saying nothing. All the places selling food were open; all the other shops were closed. I bought *hamentashen* for Liz and her family at a deserted bakery: the two women who worked there sat, ashen, listening to the radio. I bought food for the train at the Japanese grocery. On the elevator up to the market, I saw a man put his thumb and forefinger on the bridge of his nose, as if he were crying. My own eyes filled with tears. We got off the elevator: a ruddy teenager in the shop was joking with his friends in Japanese. Who did he think he was? And yet I almost wept again, paying for my sushi, because it was shocking to do something so ordinary. Because I got to have my life; because that teenager got to have his.

On the subway platform, I overheard three people who had been evacuated from World Trade Center Seven, which had collapsed a few hours later. An island of disbelief inside me shrank as they talked among themselves. *It really happened.*

I was on the first train to leave in hours. Tired people filled the seats and aisles, treating each other gently. When we pulled out of the Hudson River tunnel, first everyone turned left, to stare at the cloud rising over downtown. Then the men on either side of me took out their phones.

I heard a man say, *Never did the sky look so blue.*

The smoke column was black and vast. By Newark it had lost its brainy edges, and by Elizabeth, it was a blurred gray smear reaching half across the sky.

I heard a man say, *Stay in Panama as long as you can. And keep your World Trade Center Pass. You can show it to your grandchildren.*

Sharon met me at the station with Liz's husband Tom. Desperately relieved, I cupped her dainty face and I stroked her long brows. I touched her warm neck and I kissed her brilliant mouth. And I held and held her. We were so lucky to be alive it was embarrassing.

September 11
Veronica's Veil

Stunned and inefficient, but grateful for the task, we made a salad for dinner with Liz and Tom and their three sons. Sam, at ten, was meditative and courteous. David, at eight, wanted to know, *Why didn't they evacuate the south tower once the north tower got hit? How many people were in there?*

Isaac, the six-year-old, had had a stroke three years before. *Purple is my favorite color,* he announced periodically. Or, reaching vaguely for me, he'd say, *Your shirt is soft.*

We took hands and Liz's family said a quick grace in Hebrew over the soup, salad, cheese, bread. My eyes welled up again. *We are the ones who turn food into heat,* I thought. *We are the living.*

Liz said, *What we need to do now is understand what it is about this country that makes other people hate us so much, to see if there's some other way we can be in the world.*

When the children went to sleep, we watched the late news. Peter Jennings tripped over himself, exhausted. The buildings exploded again and again on replay; clouds of paper fluttered from the blooming flames. *That's all asbestos insulation in there,* Tom muttered. Blocks of paper and mud. The first two hundred firefighters who'd arrived on the scene were dead. Tom Brokaw was stuck in London, where it was early Wednesday morning. He held up five or six British early papers for the camera, one at a time. And five or six times there they were, just as I'd seen them out the window: the burning towers and the black coils of smoke.

The island of disbelief inside me vanished. I didn't make it up. This was no New York mass hysteria. What we saw was real, was photographable, was being seen around the world. I sobbed.

It was appalling to me that somewhere in the world it wasn't Tuesday anymore.

September 12

Wednesday Morning

Liz showed us their garden and their tree house, and Sharon introduced me to her scholar colleagues at lunch. One of them said something that upset me.

When we walked to the train station, I said, *I want to go down there. I want to see it with my own eyes.*

Me too.

We waited on the train station bench. There was a station announcement that trains were delayed. We looked at one another, terrified. Then, with a chilling lack of euphemism, they announced that trains were stalled because of a suicide due to yesterday's events. We experienced the horror of being relieved that only one person had died.

It was warm outside. In the panic of the day before—though I did think to bring her toothbrush and her nail file—I had remembered two changes of clothing for myself and none for Sharon. We sat in my sundresses and watched the pecking sparrows. In the thicket on the far side of the tracks, a rabbit lollopped towards us. It was the month for monarch butterflies. They rose up from the ivy; they danced drunken circles around each other in the light.

September 12
Engine 1, Ladder 24

The train announcer came on. *We're not collecting revenue due to the situation.*

I held Sharon when we reached Elizabeth. The smoke hadn't vanished in the night. The towers hadn't come back. *They were how I knew where the city started,* she said. *Now I can't tell what's Manhattan and what's New Jersey.*

In Penn Station, we bought World Trade Center postcards at a souvenir shop. Every statue, every key-chain, every innocent snow globe announced loss, loss, white plastic snow falling over the two towers. I gave the shopkeeper my money and we looked steadily into each other's eyes without speaking or smiling.

Sharon said, *Can you believe that when I walked through this station only yesterday, none of this had happened yet?*

No.

Me neither.

On the escalator up to the street, we smelled a breath of it: burnt plastic, asbestos, death.

Once on a sidewalk on the Upper East Side, I saw a terse record of a small disaster: a broken orange headlight and a wooden clog, like those Dr. Scholl's sandals. And then I saw this, five or ten shaken steps later: a second wooden sandal, split in half. *What kind of impact?* I wondered. *What kind of terror?*

We walked up Thirty-first Street from Penn Station and saw a fire truck parked in the street, covered in gray-white ash. The mirror and headlights were broken. Small chunks of concrete pooled on every horizontal surface, and ash filmed all the windows. People had written in the ash with their fingertips, messages in English, Spanish,

Korean. And then we saw this: a piece of poster-board with eight photographs of dead or missing men.

They smiled in the photos in their firefighter ponchos, black and green. Thomas Farino, Danny Brethel, Andy Desperito, Mike Weinberg, Steve Belson, Bill Henry. A firefighter chaplain, Father Mychal Judge. *People died.*

September 12
The New World

Home, we couldn't bear to stay inside. We took scarves to tie over our faces and went out: to try to give blood at Saint Vincent's, to try to offer help at Chelsea Piers.

They couldn't use our blood. They didn't need our help. Outside the improvised Chelsea triage center, a row of empty ambulances stood useless.

If I couldn't help, at least I wanted to witness what was happening. My self as I knew me had gone missing. I was no one. I was a city. I was a bubble in a wave of shock and grief.

Look, now the Empire State Building looks so tall, I said. *And imagine, it was built during the Depression.*

This is, literally, barbarism. They've turned back the clock so that our tallest building went up seventy years ago, said Sharon.

On walls, on mailboxes, on phone booths, we saw the first handmade signs: a photograph and a description, copied on eight-and-a-half by eleven:

Help us find Joe Ciardi
Works for Marsh & McLennan
Age: 22 HT: 5'9"
Medium Build
Brown Eyes, Hair

Have you seen Paul Radke?
Brown hair, brown eyes
5'9" 150 lbs, slim build
Appendectomy scar
Small black mole in middle of back,
Birthmark on shoulder

Evelyn Jones
Her only son is looking for his mom
If you have seen her
Please call

These signs are like tombstones, said Sharon.

The families have made the city over into a graveyard.

You'd need to, she said. *There's never going to be a body.*

The smoke was thick by the river. We walked south until we couldn't breathe, then gave up trying to get any closer. By the pink light of a perfect sunset on the West Side Highway, we joined the crowds of people hailing the rescue workers. *Thank you. Thank you.*

We talked about our friend Anita, a social worker-turned-firefighter. Intuitive, raucous, strong as an ox, compassionate and quick to cry. Her Harley, her Dalmatians, her big red truck. *I wish we could talk to her,* I said. *If she were here, I'd feel better.*

If she were here, she'd be downtown.

Mayor Giuliani urged us to stand up against hate and support Muslim New Yorkers. The *Village Voice* cover blared, *THE BAS-TARDS!* Where had we landed?

We joined Jennifer in the West Village. She'd been scheduled for a meeting at the World Trade Center on Tuesday at eleven. We ate as we walked, sometimes inhaling pizza grease and foul smoke in the same breath. *You should stay over,* said Sharon. *We have an air filter.*

We walked and walked, looking for other friends, looking for a television. *Let's sit down at a Middle Eastern place,* said Jennifer. *They must all be terrified.* We found a falafel place with a television and ate baklava. The place was deserted; the man at the counter, grave; the baklava, delicious.

September 13

Resilience

Thursday morning the wind shifted; the smoke blew up through the city instead of out toward the water. The smoke river poured toward us, its safe blue banks east and west.

After Jennifer left, we pretended to work. With all the windows shut and the air conditioner on, the air filter running, Sharon read in her office and I, unable to even try, talked on the phone. I couldn't reach my sister in Zimbabwe. *I told her you're all right,* said my mother. Two of her siblings lived in the area; she had only heard from one.

We passed our INS interview, said Cassy. *It was right down at City Hall, but it was on Monday. Can you imagine?*

Everybody's okay, said Katrin, *but I got a call from Bettina. You know she lives in Tribeca? She and Frank have been evacuated.*

I walked around like a sleepwalker, said Melissa. *I wondered when I would start crying. Not until I heard about those kids in Texas shooting out the mosque windows.*

Coughing, I could feel the razor threads of smoke shimmy in though the cracks between the windows, squirm in through the air conditioner like sperm through a prom queen's dress.

There's no point. Let's get away from here. We can try to find some blue sky.

Jennifer went to work, but she got evacuated, said Sharon. *Bomb threat.*

Maybe we can get some facemasks and try to go give blood.

They were giving masks away at the clinic on the corner, white with rubber straps, a band of metal to bend along the bridge of the nose.

Schools were closed. Shops were closed. There was no traffic allowed below Fourteenth Street. *I always dreamed of a Manhattan without cars,* said Sharon, *but this is creepy.*

I used to wish all men in suits would die, I said, coughing, *but this is unspeakable.*

Walking down the center of the deserted street, we passed three little girls, each wearing her white dust mask, playing jump rope in the late summer light.

September 13

Rule 434

Vasantha Kumal
23 yrs old
5'6" 115 lbs
D.O.B. 8/17/78

Missing loved one
Sally Lo
Height 5'7"
Weight 130 lbs
Worked for Marsh and McLennan
on the 99th floor, Tower 1.

Note: has tattoo of dragon
down the middle of back
with a Chinese character in red.
Also has a tribal tattoo
along center lower back
above tailbone.
If you have any information
on her whereabouts,
please call.

We saw the first memorial in Washington Square as we walked toward Jennifer's West Village apartment, following a band of blue sky. In the chain link fence surrounding Washington Arch, people had left flowers. There were dozens of Missing signs, scores of candles. A quote from Gandhi. A quote from Chief Seattle. Someone had left big sheets of poster-board and a pen on the fence. I wanted to leave something, but a knot of shock, of grief, stopped up my throat. *Peace on Earth,* I wrote.

I watched a young bike messenger take a sheet of paper and weave it into the chain link fence. It was a half-burned memo that had fluttered from the towers. *New Rule 434: Required Submissions of Requests For Extension of Time.*

> *I request an extension of time for Vasantha Kumal.*
>
> *I request an extension of time for Sally Lo.*

I touched the scorched edges of the paper, amber, brittle as moth wings. The bike messenger pedaled south again.

September 13

At Washington Arch

A woman tapped my shoulder. *Hi, we're doing a video project and we wanted to ask if you'd be willing to be interviewed. We're looking for whatever positive stories people have been able to find in this tragedy.*

Is this for your church? said Sharon, pointing to the woman's *One Light* T-shirt.

No, we're just interested in spirituality, said the woman.

Part of me wanted to roll my eyes, but a bigger part of me took off my facemask. *I am incredibly lucky to be alive*, I said, *and incredibly lucky not to have lost anyone personally. But we are all grieving. I am afraid of another attack here, but I am more afraid now of what our country could do to thousands of innocent people abroad. We need, not to retaliate in kind, but to reflect as a nation on how this could have happened to us, on where, in serving our own interests, we have intervened and where we have failed to intervene.*

In the paper people are saying that now we know how Israel feels, as if only the suffering of our allies merited compassion. Nagasaki, Hiroshima, My Lai, Iraq: now we know how it feels to see innocent people die.

So many of us feel helpless. We've tried to give blood, and been turned away. We've tried to volunteer, and been turned away. Last night, it was gratifying to go cheer on the rescue workers by the West Side Highway. It was nothing, really, but it felt like something. Please go film that if you have time.

We did, said the woman. *It's really inspiring. And we just wanted to ask one thing: why did you come down here today?*

I forgot to say, *To go find our friend who got evacuated.* I forgot to say, *Because I couldn't breathe.* I said, *Because we need to ask ourselves, Is what I'm doing worthwhile to me or to anyone else? And if not, maybe we should ask ourselves, What should I be doing instead? Okay, that's all. Thanks for listening.* I was blushing.

My televangelist, said Sharon proudly, as we walked away.

September 13

Gleanings from the Thursday City

We reached Jennifer's and watched her TV. *Was it always this blurry?*

Only since Tuesday, she said. *And now I can only get CBS. The other stations were transmitting from the World Trade Center.*

They thought they'd saved five people from the wreckage, but it was five rescue workers who'd gone in hours before. The debris settled with a heaving groan and people ran in panic. Blood banks were still turning people away. There was a call for boots, clothes, and bandages at Pier Forty in Tribeca.

I dunked chips in a jar of salsa, inhaling smoke. *This is what food will taste like now.*

We walked outside. On Hudson Street: a small drift of ash and broken glass.

Giuliani said that they're going to arrest anyone who preys on the people of New York by price gouging, said Jennifer. *I like that.*

Yeah, said Sharon. *My favorite was when he said that anyone who thinks making bomb threats is funny will go to jail.*

Ninety confirmed bomb threats and no bombs! I love New York: ninety psycho nut-jobs and no one evil enough to follow through.

Are you angry yet? I'm kind of numb.

Me too.

Same here.

I checked out Bin Laden online, said Sharon. *He's the last son of the last wife of a Saudi Arabian construction magnate. He has a background in structural engineering.*

So buildings are who he is, I said. *If it's him.*

What's his sign? asked Jennifer.

He doesn't give out his birthday.

We brought clothing to Pier 40. We brought bottled water to the Red Cross. We followed the sliver of blue sky until we couldn't find it, and then, breathing shallowly, we walked toward home.

September 13

My Spin Doctorate

On Sixth Avenue, the first posters: stars and stripes, *America Under Attack!*

And on the chain link fence when we passed Washington Arch again, we saw someone had cut yellow plastic Hawaiian leis and tied them to each fencepost: those Gulf War yellow ribbons all over again.

Already, someone has decided how we're supposed to experience this, I thought, sickened. And then I understood Loudi, who works at a cable access station. When we'd spoken that morning, she said she'd spent all Tuesday letting people know about alternative sources of information, reading off headlines from websites from other countries, just to broadcast a voice besides CNN. *Sharon,* I said through my facemask, *let's do something. I want to walk down the street and see what I believe. Let's make stickers.*

Over tea, I wrote out what I could remember of what I'd said to the video people. *It's great, but it's too long,* said Sharon. *How about this: 'They think we're monsters too. Let's prove them wrong.'*

Okay. And one that says 'Justice without slaughter.'

I made them, I printed them on sticker paper, I cut them up, and we walked around the block that night, to give ourselves, if no one else, something else to look at.

It was nothing, but it felt like something.

September 14

The Cruelest Day

We woke to rain. *The rest of Manhattan won't catch fire now,* I thought, *but the rubble will be heavier.* Pouring water on a campfire makes it smoke: I thought about people trapped under the buildings, dying of smoke inhalation. I thought about two hundred and twenty floors' worth of asbestos drizzling out to sea, working its way up the food chain. I went back to sleep.

Sharon worked at home that morning, and I made phone calls. I called old lovers, or called friends they still talked to. I called to find out about my uncle on Long Island. My cousin said they were all fine, but named more missing from her town than I could let myself hear. She mentioned Nostradamus; we had both seen the same TV special as children. And here it was, as frightening as poetry: a sea of ghost ships. A sea of empty cars in commuter lots, long after midnight on Tuesday.

Then I called my uncle who lives in Connecticut. I heard unspeakable loss in the soft way he asked, *Are you getting everything you need down there? Bottled water?*

We went to the Quaker meeting house at noon, but it was closed. A sign directed us to the Episcopal church next door.

Everyone approaches God in their own way, said the minister. He was hoarse, and asked someone else to lead the song, *My Country 'Tis of Thee.* The words were soap and ashes in my mouth, but I sang. And then I wept in my pew, because I searched in my heart and heard no God.

I had believed, until then, in that Quaker divine spark in each person, but I hadn't thought that was God in his or her entirety. But with desperate clarity I saw how small a spark is, a thing doused with wet fingers. A thing crushed underfoot. I saw what Annie Dillard sees: a tiny God, a brittle God, a moth, helpless but for our crude and preoccupied hands.

The minister invited people to stand and speak, if they wished. A woman started preaching, *The Risen Christ, The Risen Christ, The Risen Christ.* We left.

When we walked outside, it was raining. There was a green wall that looked fresh and wet against the silty sky. *Pretty,* I said.

Remember that miso *cod we had at Nobu? Their 'signature hot dish?'*

The taste of salt cod and sweet *miso* belonged to a world I could only picture as if through the wrong side of a pair of binoculars. *You want to try to make that again?*

Well, not today, said Sharon. She was quiet for a long moment. *But those* hamentashen *you brought to Princeton were good. Where'd you get them?*

Moishe's, down the street

Really?

Moishe's was open. The two women, gray and silent on Tuesday, were talking again today, weighing cookies and opening bags.

I didn't know Moishe's was so good. Remember that big dusty cookie of theirs Neil brought us? That was not their 'signature hot dish.'

I laughed out loud for the first time in three days, as a black SUV made an abrupt and sloppy turn onto our street.

Hey, watch out for pedestrians! Sharon shook her fist.

I guess they're letting traffic below Fourteenth Street, I said.

April is the cruelest month, you'll see, in large italic type, floating across the pages of every spring catalog: Godiva, Victoria's Secret, J. Crew. Do they care what it means?

It's the Friday after the world ended on a Tuesday.

It's this: wincing back to life again.

September 14

Every Broken Thing Made Whole

Sharon made grilled cheese sandwiches and we met Jennifer at the blood bank. *By appointment only,* the sign said. We took the bus downtown again and brought candles to Tompkins Square Park for a vigil. We saw a child on our way, holding a candle as she read on her stoop.

We stood quiet in the rising night, one or two hundred people, candles in hand, loosely gathered around a candle burning on the ground. We were uneasy, abashed, private in our grief and uncertain en masse. What were we supposed to do? Our candles felt inadequate, excessive, precious. Then a red-haired man in a white chef's jacket, apparently on break from work, moved into the center, solemnly left his candle, and stole away. I thought about the people at Windows on the World, the cooks, the waiters, the dishwashers, out of a job or dead. Someone sighed. A woman went to the center and quietly left her candle. The repeated gesture gathered us: now we knew what to do.

As one by one we approached the center, the cluster of candles grew into a mandala, an island, a small city, brilliantly lit, a skyline aflame, but not in danger. I wished somebody would start a song. My body longed to be buoyed up with singing. *By the waters of Babylon, we lay down and wept for thee, Zion. Dona nobis pacem, dona nobis pacem, dona nobis pacem.* I could think of dozens of love songs and only one prayer, only one lament. *Give us peace. We lay down and wept.*

September 15

Numb

On Saturday morning, while Sharon was in the shower, Jennifer called to say they were collecting supplies for firefighters at Our Lady of Pompeii in her neighborhood. *They said that the firefighters are really touched when they get homemade stuff,* she said. *I think I'm going to bake some cookies.*

At that moment, the idea of baking cookies for firefighters seemed so hopeless, so girly, it made me want to crawl into a hole and hide.

I wanted to be alone. Sara and I had a sort-of date for tea ceremony on Sunday, so I bought sweets in Chinatown. The man at the store tried to give me an American flag. Outside, on Canal Street, I saw the first T-shirts: *America Fights Back. I survived the World Trade Center.*

No cars were allowed below Canal Street. I had to pass a police barricade to reach the Taiwanese tea place I liked. In a storefront Buddhist temple, I burned a stick of incense. I watched, lumpish, as the smoke struggled through the leaden air.

It was the first time since Tuesday that Sharon and I had been separated, I realized. Anything could have happened to her. The first twelve pay phones I tried didn't work, and when I finally got through, she wasn't there.

I went home. Sara called to say she couldn't come for tea on Sunday after all.

I did some work, finally. I sank into the snowy arms of work.

Catholic cathedrals, like even tiny storefront Buddhist temples, offer side altars leading to a main chamber. In cathedrals, these are saints' altars—Joseph with a staff, Agnes with a lamb, Lucy with her eyes on a plate—to which pilgrims bring special petitions. For selling

---

houses, they go to Joseph; for journeys, to Christopher; for hopeless cases, to Jude.

My world has contracted to a temple to this horror, in which I circle from altar to altar. All the pantheon is here: one who weeps, one who rages, one who tries to help. One who laughs again. One who wants to die. Today I burn incense for the one who cannot read the paper, for the one who cannot hope.

September 16

A Palliative

Sunday morning felt like Saturday all over again. I sat on the couch, staring at the column of smoke out the window, white now instead of black. Sharon played the new Björk CD: It felt like a time capsule, a quaint snapshot of the tiny world before Tuesday. *I don't think I can bear to hear that. Sorry.*

So, what do you want to do?

Nothing.

Can we eat those sweets you bought yesterday?

Oh, let's do tea ceremony. It'll be nice to not think for an hour.

I folded up the futon, oiled the wood, and wiped down the *tatami*. I asked Sharon to find some flowers and she hung basil from her window box in a vase on the wall. We sat on the *tatami* floor, grassy and fragrant, and I served her sweets. I set out a bamboo teaspoon and a lacquer box. I drew hot water with a bamboo dipper and poured it into a tea bowl. I dipped a new bamboo tea whisk in that water: it opened like a flower, its curved ends unfurling in the wet heat. I threw away the water and wiped the tea bowl with a linen cloth. Inside the lacquer box was a soft hill of brilliant green powdered tea. I scooped some into the bowl, and while Sharon ate her sweets, I added hot water and whisked the tea and water into a foamy broth. Sharon drank it, and I made some for myself, cutting the sticky, loamy sweets with the bitter frothy tea.

And, just as carefully, I cleaned everything again and carried it away. I offered a prayer to Kannon, Kuan Yin, the goddess of mercy. The trees blazed green outside, making sugar out of light, exhaling clean air.

Some people went to movies that weekend, some people went to the gym to pound their grief away. *The New York Times* said *The world of sports—a palliative for many Americans—was unavailable,* as most events were canceled until Monday.

Let's go to the park, said Sharon. *I liked that Audre Lorde quote you put on the wall.*

We must learn to count the living with that same particular attention with which we number the dead.

September 16
Silent Spring

The Missing signs—the faces of the dead—were harder to spot on the Upper East Side, but so were the faces of the living. We rode the bus past dozens, hundreds of shops, all closed. The things of this world—the opals, coats, and cashmere, the leather boots and silver salvers—were not for sale today. *I hope it's only because this is Sunday,* said Sharon. *These people can't afford to be closed all week.*

We went to Central Park and sat on a rock. Sharon read; I held her around the waist and sat quietly, looking at the sun in the oak leaves, the scattered acorns. I took deep breaths of clear air. Children rollerbladed, adults napped or sketched. Bird droppings spattered to the ground a few feet away.

Hey, I just heard a fire truck without panicking, said Sharon.

That's a first, I agreed.

On Broadway, a marquee announced a cancelled concert. Fairway Market thronged with people who had finally found the heart to buy vegetables. Out one ear, I heard a woman say, *Everything's up in the air.* Out the other, I heard, *Everything's on hold.* When Sara had called to cancel, she'd said, *Everything's moment to moment. I can't make any plans.*

September 16

Union Square

We took the bus downtown with our groceries and got off at Fourteenth Street. Union Square was alive with grief. Hundreds of people wandered in the late warm sun, lighting candles, leaving flowers, reading the posters of the mourned and missing.

> Patrick Michael Keenan—Known as Ricky
> March 23, 1964 6'0" 180 lbs
> Eyes: brown Hair: strawberry blonde
> A silver ring on the 4th finger of each hand.
> Please call

> Mr. Kenjiro Sato
> Hair: Black
> Eyes: Brown
> Height: 5 Feet 7 Inch
> He usually wears glasses.
> He wears braces on his teeth for orthopedics.
> Japanese
> If you find him, please call

Anupa Bannerjee
and Raj Singh
age 26 and 36 years
working at computer help desk/
working as director, audio visual
Marsh & McLennan
please call Anil

Ricky grinned in his glasses, Mr. Sato held his daughter, Raj and Anupa stood together smiling.

Beth Roberts is missing.

Jimmy Glynne is missing.

Flocks of children's drawings perched on wire fences: every classroom in New York had witnessed this. People left photographs and poems. They left dolls and bibles and baseball caps. They posted signs.

An eye for an eye makes the whole world blind.

Our grief is not a cry for war.

At the base of the park, a woman stood on a chair, speaking against both hate crimes at home and bombing abroad. She was dressed as the Statue of Liberty and painted a monochrome green. Nearby, a guitarist played for a circle of listeners. Past him, a jazz group fanned the air into a sweet, aching breeze, and beyond them, we heard chanting.

Tibetans had come to mourn, and to pray for peace. Fifty or sixty sat together, surrounding a forest of burning incense and candles, turning pages in their prayer-books, reading right to left. We sat down behind them, our arms around each other, borne up by the rising net of sound. They sang. *They sang.*

I once asked Katrin about the white silk cloth draped on Buddha statues on Tibetan altars. You see it on doors to Tibetan restaurants, too, and Brad Pitt's hosts gave him white cloths at the end of *Seven Years in Tibet.* She told me, *It's called a* kata. *They give them to their Lamas.* There was a fencepost knotted high with *katas* at the heart of the chanting chorus.

Sharon sighed. *They've suffered so much and they still advocate non-violence.*

I bowed my head and felt their singing voices buzz inside my chest.

September 16

Communion

We went home and made love for the first time in a week. She was a gold suede horse. Hand over hand, my braided rope. My moon. My own. My odalisque. She shuddered into flight and then we wept.

They were with us, the missing thousands, the photos in their eight-and-a-half by eleven frames of ghostly white. Sally with her little dog, Vasantha in her graduation gown, holding lilies. Jimmy, Beth, Evelyn, Paul. Flat rectangle ghosts, trembling in the beaten air. Helpless in their wedding photos, helpless in their shirts and sweaters, helpless as they held their children. The dead of eighty nations. The dead of every color. The dead we still called *missing*, holding us in their surprise and terror as we, desperately, held them.

I could see their faces, Sharon.

Me too. And then she said a minute later, *We have to do something.*

September 17
Monday Radio

They said their FM transmitter had been located on the World Trade Center.

They said that on the 1/9 and N/R subway lines, Rector Street and Cortland Street were closed indefinitely as stations are flooded or destroyed.

They said there was a two-hour delay on the Lincoln Tunnel.

They said that the stock market opens again today at 9:30.

They said the Mets play Pittsburgh tonight.

They said that the US might lift a ban on participation in international assassinations.

They said that Iran had closed its border to Afghan refugees.

They said Bush announced that the Taliban would face air strikes if Bin Laden were not turned over.

They said that because of the recent civil war, there were no high-value targets left in Afghanistan.

They said that thousands of paratroopers had been mobilized.

They said that alternate-side-of-the-street parking regulations had been suspended.

They said no one had been found alive since Wednesday.

September 17

Something

The radio played its first commercials since Tuesday, sometimes simultaneously, to make up for lost time. Beyond the Babel Tower of better window treatments and better car alarms, the white pillar of cloud rose over downtown.

Sharon went to Princeton, mostly to fight her fear of being separated again, her fear of traveling at all. She forwarded email letters she'd sent the president and senators, one from Saturday, one from Sunday, one from that morning.

I made postcards. On one side, I wrote a letter, addressed to the president:

I am a New Yorker who has witnessed the atrocity of an attack on ordinary citizens. I ask you to bring the perpetrators to justice without endangering the lives of innocent people.

I added the White House email and phone numbers. On the other side, I listed email addresses for our senators, for NBC, CBS, CNN, *USA Today*, *The New York Times*. *Tell the world to go to Union Square and see for themselves: New York wants justice, not slaughter.*

I took my originals to Santo's copy shop and had them printed on cardstock, brilliant spring green. Santo looked them over and gave me half off, nodding. *Leave some for me to give people here*, he said. I bought stamps. I bought scotch tape.

A young man, not a big reader, followed me. *What's with, like, slaughter?*

I looked up, shy. *What happened here shouldn't happen anywhere, you know?*

Yeah, and in the Gulf War we killed all those people and we didn't get the guy. I don't want to get drafted if we can't get the guy.

I know, I said, rolling my eyes. *He could be in Monaco. He could be here.*

He's in Atlantic City, he said. *He's at the Taj.*

September 17

The Key of Dreams

My friends had all been too stunned to meet up, but on Monday night at last I joined Katrin, who worked on Union Square. *It looked so close on Tuesday,* she said. *We were all so afraid.* Her arms were sore: she'd spent seven hours the night before volunteering at the Salvation Army. *Wendy and I carried boxes and made up packages of stuff for the firefighters. I boxed up more mini-muffins last night than I ever care to see in my life. But it was good to feel bone-tired from* doing *something instead of feeling so helpless and insomniac.*

I hear you. How have your dreams been?

I haven't been remembering them, she said. *I've just had little snatches of sleep here and there. It's probably good I can't remember them. What about you?*

Total escapism: a house full of sleeping kittens. And National Geographic-*style dreams: The Beautiful Continent of Africa. The Beautiful Islands of Aleutia. And then I wake up, and it's a nightmare.*

Yep. Someone should catalog these dreams.

We went to Benny's Burritos in the West Village with her roommate Wendy and Wendy's friend Todd. The waiters there, as everywhere this week, were eerily kind.

Is there anything you can do about that painting? We asked. Directly over our table hung a large canvas of a city at night, with a plane flying low overhead, its blunt nose aimed straight for the viewer.

The waiter looked embarrassed. *We talked to the manager about it last night.*

September 18
Notes from the Week After

Tuesday morning, fifty-four hundred missing, 215 officially dead. A scummy haze out my window where the towers used to be. The United States asked Pakistan to ask the Taliban to turn over Bin Laden. The Taliban is turning the question over to a group of Islamic scholars. (*Do they even know where he is?* I asked aloud.) The Mets won against Pittsburgh. Light and variable winds, a high of seventy-eight.

The radio asked if I felt sad or empty. If I had difficulty going about my daily routine. If I had trouble falling asleep. It was an ad for antidepressants.

Kathy told me that a guy on her friend Melody's train started abusing a Middle Eastern man. *Stop! Stop!* screamed Melody, pointing at the bully. *Get that man off the train!* The other passengers banded together and got the Middle Eastern man safely off the train. But why couldn't they have charged the thug instead?

This week: an email from my editor. A phone call from Africa, and one from France. Two calls from Japan. A card from San Francisco: *It is so upsetting to see the tragedy, and I can't do anything. I hope you are fine. I tried to call you, but all circuits are busy.*

We gathered at the little Statue of Liberty, said my friend Lisa in Paris. *We held a vigil.*

My sister, in Zimbabwe, said she saw pictures of the falling bodies in a magazine. In Mexico, too, they saw those pictures.

Not here, I said.

We gave the Taliban forty-three million dollars last year as a reward for cracking down on the opium trade.

Was the Taliban elected?

No. They rose up and took over.

(By the way, was Hitler elected?

Not by the German people. He was appointed Chancellor by a weak president, then terrorized a body of lawmakers into voting him dictator.)

A rumor circulating in the Arab world: Israel knew about, or planned, the attacks and told four thousand Jews to stay home from work that Tuesday.

They're sad they didn't see more Jews burn, said Sharon.

The footage of Palestinian children dancing in the street after the attacks was actually from the Gulf War, some said. Others claimed it was from Tuesday.

One of the guys who fought the attackers in the plane that came down in Pennsylvania was a gay rugby player from San Francisco, said Sharon. *Anita told me.*

It never gets in the news when a gay person does something good, I complained.

Jerry Falwell, who had claimed that the terrorist attack was God's punishment on America for supporting gay and abortion rights, apologized today.

The first signs came out that weren't about the attacks:

Wanted: guitarist and more.

Lost cockatiel: answers to "Omar."

This has been the longest week in my life, I wrote, *and yet I've done nothing, except get older.*

How do you teach six and a half billion people to value each other?

This week, Palestinian-American poet Suheir Hammad, in a piece called *first writing since:*

Over there is over here.

Grief has restrung us, new gut for old steel.

September 18

The Looters

Why record this?

(At lunch, in Princeton, on September 12, Sharon's colleague said, *Maybe I can get something out of this.* Monster. Mirror. I looked away.)

Because I was here.

September 18

Scoop

I went to Union Square on Tuesday and taped up more of my green postcards. Hundreds of people filed quietly past the photographs, candles, flowers, and posters, adding writing of their own. I worked slowly, my eyes tearing up sometimes, reading the signs people had left.

> Missing
> Port Authority Police Officer
> Umoja "Django" Richards
> Badge #811
> If you have seen him,
> please contact his wife Gwen.

> Looking for bestfriend
> Abu Hassan
> Espeed/Cantor, 112th floor
> Can anyone who knows him or
> anything about him
> Please contact me at any of these
> numbers or email
> He has been the best friend with a
> heart of gold
> I've ever had when I lived in N.Y.
> Please help me to find out!

People asked me for cards to give to their friends. A reporter from a Japanese daily paper asked how many cards I had made. *Four hundred yesterday, eight hundred today.*

Why did you make them?

Because I think we have a very narrow margin of time to make our voices heard before our country starts bombing Afghanistan and killing civilians.

We need to take Bin Laden to court, she agreed.

A journalism student from the New School asked me about the postcards too. *What organization are you from?*

I did this myself, I said. *I'm an American; for better or worse I don't trust organizations. I wanted to give people something they could do without being part of a group.*

What do you think should be done?

If I were in charge? I think we should pay our UN dues, apprehend Bin Laden and his top people, and try them in World Court. As myself? I think we should infiltrate his organization and off everyone with any power.

Maybe the Mob could do it, she said. *Or the Russian Mafia, the Columbian drug cartels.*

Exactly! This isn't a war, this is organized crime.

Yeah, if it were a war, Bin Laden would care whether innocent people were killed. But there are five hundred Muslims missing from the attacks. He's responsible to no group of people, to no country, to no source of profit, even. Not even to his followers: they're willing to die.

My girlfriend Sharon said we should sue him.

Wow.

Imagine if all the ambulance-chasing lawyers in New York got together?

That's brilliant.

I kept taping up cards and kept reading, breathing in the smell of candles and burning buildings. Hairdressers were cutting hair to raise money for the victims. Comedians were hosting joke nights. We hadn't turned overnight into doctors or firefighters, much as we might have wished it. We were, again, simply ourselves, only more so.

A sign said

There were eight million stories in the naked city.
Now there's one.

I saw a CNN reporter and gave him a postcard. *Thanks,* he said absently. He talked to the camera about plans for possible United States air strikes and added that information had been discovered indicating that terrorists had planned or were still planning another attack of some kind for Saturday, September 22.

Most of my cards from Monday had vanished, I noticed, but a few remained. Someone had defaced them: *Simple Simon. Unrealistic. Yeah right. War for Peace.* I took them down, disheartened, and replaced them with new cards. *It isn't all in vain,* I thought, watching a woman pause and take a card from the wall. I walked home, past the faces of Beth, Abu, Django, Raj. I saw, still looped in the fence, a white silk *kata.* I was tempted, briefly, to take it, but I touched it instead.

September 18

Some Background

Sharon is in New York with me this year because she's on leave: usually she teaches in the Bay Area. She had planned to hold on to her San Francisco apartment for the year, because it was cheap and rent-controlled, but when her landlords started calling and giving her trouble in early September, she decided to let it go and gave notice. She needed to be out by the end of the month.

On Tuesday morning, a week after the attacks, we had decided to stick with our plans: on Saturday, she would fly to San Francisco to pack up her apartment and I would stay home and see old friends. But on Tuesday night when I told her what the CNN reporter had said—that another attack had been planned for Saturday—her small body coiled in panic. She thought volubly about what to do next, her shoes ticking back and forth across the apartment. *I'll go by train*, she announced.

I'll come with you.

September 19

Pilgrimage

My friend Bremner flew in from Paris on Monday night. He'd had a concert to give in New York, and, even more, he wanted to see the city for himself. For days the smoke had been too thick for me to go far downtown, but on Wednesday morning it was the faintest smear on the southern horizon. As I squinted at the smoke, Bremner called from his hotel. *They let me walk straight down Broadway,* he said. *It was awful, but I had to do it.*

I took the subway to Canal Street and approached the police barricade on a side street. They asked me for ID, and I timidly backed away. I tried again on Broadway. *Why are you coming down here?* they asked, when I showed my driver's license.

Because I want to see what happened. I want to pay my respects.

I was white, well dressed, a woman. He said, *If anybody asks, tell them you came down to shop,* and waved me through.

The empty downtown streets were silent—no cars, no people— but I could see a crowd farther south. I wondered where, if asked, I should say I was shopping. Wasn't Century 21 gone?

Because I had once dated a woman who lived in Jersey City, I'd been through the World Trade Center subway station many times: I remembered a dull tile mosaic of blue, green, and brown coins. And I remembered a dozen escalators side by side. I'd once seen them in a movie like *Koyaanisqatsi:* hundreds of people filing up and down the escalators in sped-up motion, intercut with hundreds of slaughterhouse chickens on sped-up conveyor belts. Under millions of tons of rubble, was the mosaic still standing? Had people died on those escalators?

Aside from commuting, aside from my first dizzy ascent five years before, I had been to the World Trade Center only one other time: to buy a bra that fit. To get six of the same bra from Victoria's Secret, I had taken subways to nine of their stores throughout Manhattan. One of many dead ends had been their shop in the mall under the World Trade Center, which, I'd learned the hard way, had not yet opened for business. I remembered trudging past soaped and papered windows and taking the N/R home.

And that store, *that very store*, I read, had since opened and was intact, a pocket cavern beneath the rubble. No one had been found there: the towers fell before opening time. Because I knew that looters had ransacked the Tourneau watch store nearby, I entertained a vision of a firefighter, headlamp ablaze, tucking filmy panties into an ash-white poncho, and laughed aloud. As I walked down Broadway toward the site, I shook my head in wonder: maybe my bra was down there somewhere.

When I could see the World Trade Center out my front windows, I had thought it was arrogant, ugly, boring. At the same time, even if I would have preferred seeing the elegant Thai headdress of the Chrysler Building every day, I had secretly liked having a recognizable piece of the New York skyline to take for granted. The World Trade Center, when I'd thought about it, was linked in my mind with the World Trade Organization: monolithic, oppressive, wrong. It was part of a global machine designed to make most people desperately poor and a few people obscenely rich. There was a reason I spent more on six bras than the woman who sewed them probably made in a year, and the World Trade Center was part of it.

Now that they were so clearly so vulnerable, I loved the two buildings. I longed to visit the ugly mosaic, the soul-deadening escalators, that temple of false choices, the mall. *But there is a reason why they chose this place, why they chose the Pentagon. Vulnerability can make a thing more endearing, but not less corrupt*, I thought. And then the faces of the dead smiled at me—they weren't machines of world conquest, they were thousands of individual precious nobodies—and I couldn't think.

I walked past City Hall and looked west at what was left.

September 19

What I Saw Downtown

It was a skeletal galleon. It was a volcanic crater. It was the mouth of hell.

It ravished my heart. It took me with it.

It was like all the photographs, but starker for being real: a pit of concrete and steel, exhaling black smoke. Here and there were wafers of grillework, many stories high, standing upright in the wreckage.

The reason those towers could climb so high, explained Bremner, *is that the outer frames of steel formed their support. Think of an exoskeleton. That's how the tissue of floors could collapse flat; that's why the towers didn't topple, but fell straight down.*

Surrounding the blocks of twisted debris rose buildings with blown-out windows, buildings sleeved in ash. Twenty stories up, I saw a building with a fallen piece of grillework caught in its flank like a dart in a board.

Keep moving, the police told us as we filed past the corpse. *Take one picture and move on.*

September 19

Rest in Peace

The soft ash, like snow underfoot. The ash on every leaf of every potted tree. Ash coating the Godiva store. A spilt cup of ash on an ash-covered counter. Ash on windows, lettered by passers-by.

Death to Bin Laden.

Meet hate with love.

76th Precinct was here.

Ash on awnings. The ash the women couldn't reach with a hose. The sweaters for sale, dripping with ash. The new boots with their ashy toes.

I craved green: green tea, my green postcards, green leaves in Central Park, the green lungs of the city.

The human lung, unfurled, is thirty feet long.

I saw the finest of threads mixed among the ash: asbestos? I touched it, just barely, with the tip of my finger. I gingerly brought my finger to my tongue.

The ash was composed of steel and concrete, of course, and of two hundred twenty floors of asbestos insulation. Of glass, of carpets, of cubicles. Of computers, of copiers, of televisions, telephones. Of elevators. Of desks and chairs and conference tables. Of restaurant ovens, bright bottles of liquor. And of the dead. I swear I tasted salt.

The dead are among us, coating the sweaters and the awnings, coating thirty feet of every lung.

September 19

A Few Words about the Bad Smell

In *A Natural History of the Senses*, Diane Ackerman discusses the delicate but potent scent of the violet, its unusual gift for stimulating the nose, then blocking its own effects, then stimulating the nose again. Which means we never get used to violets: their scent occurs to us again and again, as if for the first time, in waves.

Acrid: Bitterly pungent to the organs of taste or smell, or to the skin, etc.; irritating; corrosive.

It blew in at random, but most often, at first, after dark. *At night the air is cooler and heavier, and water vapor condenses around the particulate matter*, my scientist friend Katy told me. Later, when we smelled it during the day, she explained how land heats up faster than water, described warm air rising up from the island and cool air rushing in to take its place, death carried in on that wind.

It persisted, week after week, death worming silently into our days, into October, into November, as the rubble burned and burned. I do not know when it will end.

September 19

Derelict

I went up to Union Square again, to tape up more postcards. On Tuesday, I had gone at five, just as work was letting out, and on Wednesday I went at four, so perhaps that accounted for it, but in any case something felt different.

I started working at the edges, as I had before, and saw that the same jerk who defaced my cards on Monday had come back. My cards from Tuesday were gone, but many of the other messages urging peace had been scrawled over.

War for peace.

A woman with wild unbrushed hair and a torn-off sandal-strap asked for more of my cards, speaking very quickly. Her movements were tight and jagged. From what, political fervor? How many post-card stamps would you need to resell to get high?

Mixed in with the flowers, candles, photographs, and signs, I saw more religious leaflets than I had the day before. A man asked about my cards and invited me to join his church.

Another man paced back and forth, selling enamel flag pins. *Two dollars. Just two dollars. These colors don't run, and the people who wear these colors don't run. A gift for your family or loved one.*

I moved away from the edges to the crowded base of the square, where the pool of candles and flowers spread over dozens of feet and the statue of George Washington on his warhorse had been chalked over with peace signs.

No war! Not in our name.

I put up my cards until they were gone. A family of beautiful dark-haired women and girls took the last few. As I walked away, I saw they all had identical T-shirts: *Volunteer Minister*.

The only music in the square was a drum, which sounded every four or five seconds from the clump of dreadlocked white teenagers camped on the grass with their dogs and sleeping bags.

Only the faces of the dead, above the wilted petals and the melted wax, retained their power.

> Manuel Cervantes
> Empire Blue Cross
> and Blue Shield
> 26th floor, 1 World Trade Center
> Filipino (Asian)
> 58 Years Old. 4'11" 130 Pounds
> Salt and pepper curly hair
> Very distinctive thick brown toenails

I turned to leave for home. The *kata* was gone.

September 20
Don't Let the Left Hand Know

To take a plane, we had to go behind our own backs.

On Wednesday night, seven friends came over for dinner. It was a blessing just to see their faces. Sharon ran out to the pharmacy to get sleeping pills for our train trip. *Are you guys getting a sleeper?*

Just seats, that's why we need the pills. It's three nights, four days.

Why not?

Sharon said there was something wrong with sleepers, I can't remember.

You can't sleep three nights sitting up! Get a sleeper!

Later, I asked Sharon, *What was wrong with getting a sleeper compartment? Were they super expensive?*

No, they were booked solid for the next two weeks.

Oh.

We could make frequent flyer reservations and decide at the last minute.

Let's do that, I said.

On Thursday morning, before Sharon went out for a walk, she said, *Whether we take the plane or the train, we need to leave at noon, so let's both think about it this morning.*

At eleven, she came home. *Which is it?*

I couldn't look her in the eye. *Let's get on a plane,* I shrugged, fiddling with a bag.

Okay.

September 20
The Shrine of Rage

Before Sharon came home on Thursday morning, I packed my bags and stood at the window. The white smudge that was left of the column of smoke was invisible against the overcast sky.

I went outside. I hoped one of the many Tibetan stores in the neighborhood would have a *kata* I could leave in San Francisco, but I was out of luck. There was a *kata* on a Buddha statue, a *kata* on a fire extinguisher, but none for sale.

A soft rain was blowing down, and I looked around carefully. *What would I want to think of if I were dying?* The corner of Saint Mark's Place and Second Avenue seemed precious enough to me: red brick and sycamore trees, buildings named IDA and FLORENCE, Gem Spa, Veselka, the Ottendorfer library. The smell of grease at Dallas BBQ, the smell of coffee at Porto Rico, the iron railings, the gingko leaves, the green clematis vines reaching up the side of my building. To say nothing of the blue morning glories, twining upward with their wet green heart-shaped leaves.

I stopped to look at the morning glories: blue trumpets, blue faces, each blue blast a single throated whorl. The cool wet petals felt like thin skin, soft and taut. How could a single thing evoke a jewel, an ear, a clock, a bell, a face, stained glass? How could anything be this beautiful?

How could you see something this beautiful and want to die? How could you see this and want to kill?

You fucking bastards, how could you harden your hearts to beauty?

September 20

Rainy New Year

Once we got in the cab, I produced a handful of apple slices and a plastic honey bear. *Happy Rosh Hashanah*, I told Sharon, feeding her.

L'Shana Tova, she said with a kiss.

We drove slowly past Union Square, watching rain melt the dead faces into rags. Manuel, Manuel, toenails and all. Sharon, crying, took my hand.

It's like they're dying all over again.

Isn't it enough, to be killed and ashed and scattered?

Do we have to breathe and drink their pictures too?

Today I cannot bear the ruthless thrift of living, the sickening alchemy of rot and seed. Even grief becomes manure.

September 20

The Friendly Skies

Our cab driver missed the airport exit and backed a hundred feet up the highway without turning on his hazards. In the airport, people were checking in their bags, as always, by machine, punching in answers to security questions: *Have your bags been under your control at all times? Have any strangers asked you to carry anything on board? Bing. Bing.* As we walked through the metal detectors, I thought about all the innocent things that could, in the right hands, stab, blind, or choke: a pen, a fingernail, a shoelace.

Strapped into my seat, waiting for the plane to take off, I thought, *I now commend myself to the hard green bosom of earth.* And at the same time: *Come on! Let's get moving already!*

We tried to read the paper. Sculptor Richard Serra, a Tribeca resident, saw it out his window, saw people *fall off those buildings like feathers.*

They didn't fall like feathers, I thought, watching rain smash against the window.

This is the monument I imagined, something rain can't alter: two of the ghost shards of grillework, standing in the air, and under them, a pavement of black marble etched with the names of the dead, like the Vietnam wall. Moving across the names, a thin sheet of gleaming water, constantly washing them clean.

We held our breaths until Pittsburgh.

Undercover security? Two of our flight attendants were the biggest, burliest, straightest-looking men I'd ever seen asking *Coffee, milk, or tea?* And they were far nicer than regular flight attendants.

So many sentences since September eleventh had had the same ending, voiced or implied, sensical or non: *...because of the attacks.*

Such as: *I felt a stab of compassion for the person who had diarrhea in the airplane bathroom before me.*

September 20

Terrorism

I got an email from my friend Melissa before we left for San Francisco.

I keep feeling as though there's this person following me around, waiting patiently when I wake up each morning and quietly demanding my attention all day. That person is the knowledge that the whole world has changed. That person is fear. She's a rotten roommate.

We read through the paper and tried to breathe deeply. Sharon had brought a distraction: Haruki Murakami's book of interviews with victims of a nerve gas attack in the Tokyo subway system. *This isn't helping*, I said.

I tried to fill out a survey that a psychology student had given me on Union Square. *Are you experiencing fear? What are you afraid of?*

I'm afraid my country will kill thousands and thousands of innocent people. All the dead there will have names and faces too.

Mole at jawbone near right ear.

Thick brown toenails.

A birthmark in the shape of Puerto Rico.

And I'm afraid of nerve gas, anthrax, smallpox in the drinking water. Mass hysteria. Internment camps for Muslim Americans. War. We win by dropping the bomb and the fallout blows back and we die painfully. They win and kill the queers, stone unmarried women who have sex, all women who have jobs, all men who shave. I'm afraid that I'll look back next year and these will have been the good days, when we only had the World Trade Center to worry about. I hope I live long enough to get cancer from the asbestos.

Oh, I forgot to tell you, said Sharon. *On the train I saw this little kid who had clearly never taken the subway before. I heard him tell his parents, 'I want to take the subway forever and ever until it's destroyed.'*

Yeah? The other day, I heard this woman say, *My anthrax kit? A tub of gelato and a gun.*

September 20

Cognitive Dissonance

The San Francisco airport was deserted. A cortège of empty cabs sat idle. We sped north, then slowed down in traffic. *What's happening?* asked Sharon, taking my hand. We imagined the Transamerica Pyramid in flames, the Bay Bridge a broken necklace. Our brains made small loops that ended, *because of the attacks, because of the attacks.*

Baseball game, said the driver. We smiled weakly at each other.

We overheard kids in the Mission chanting, *Fuck the war! Fuck, fuck the war!*

We saw one or two American flags in windows, and elsewhere a sign that read

United States Out of the Middle East.

We looked at each other uncertainly. I nodded, slowly, shrugging. *I guess they have a point*, I groped. *If we'd made cars that didn't run on gasoline, or if we weren't allied with Israel…*

I think they didn't bother to make a new sign, snapped Sharon.

We set down our things in Sharon's apartment and went out to a restaurant. We stopped to get the new Tori Amos CD, and overheard the record store clerks chatting. *I never thought about 'em. Why should I miss 'em?*

A sign caught our eyes at the corner.

On the day the bombing starts, gather at Powell and Market at five PM to protest!

What makes them so sure Powell and Market will be there? Remember Giuliani's command center, inside *the World Trade Center?*

No, when we *bomb Afghanistan.*

Oh, right.

September 20

Delfina Ristorante

A dainty salad of radish and cucumbers, salty flecks of silver anchovy, tender fresh mozzarella, sweet heirloom tomatoes, basil oil.

Buttermilk panna cotta. Blackberries.

Red velvet wine.

Candles, linen, mirrors. People were talking louder than we'd heard all week. We failed to make sense of so many sentences. *I had a good workout today. Do you think he likes me, or is he just saying that? I creamed Sanders; I just annihilated him. I collect first editions.*

It's that they're talking about themselves, said Sharon.

Oh, that's it, I said.

Through my tears, it all came back: the burning buildings, the black pillars of smoke, the white ash dripping off the sweaters, the grillework standing in the wreckage, the three jump rope girls in their surgical masks, the candle city and the dead thousands; Mychal, Vasantha, Sally, Manuel.

We've seen too much, I sobbed. *We've seen too much.*

September 21

The Sun Also Rises

That night, I lay asleep beside Sharon in our bed in San Francisco. Because my dreaming body knew I wouldn't wake to breathe ashes, it stopped manufacturing kittens and scenery.

I stood on the Promenade in Brooklyn Heights, with a clear and panoramic view of Manhattan.

Every building worthy of the name was burning. The Empire State, the Chrysler, the Woolworth's, the United Nations, all of them were funneling upward in black coils of smoke. I could see the people at the windows, and the people jumping, each mouth a small desperate *o*.

It's okay, it's okay, said Sharon when I woke.

I'm afraid of dying. I'm afraid we're going to kill so many people.

We held each other.

Last night, Sharon said, *when our plane came in, did you see the fog?* I did. It was so beautiful, filling up the valley like milk, pouring out of a gap between the hills like milk down a spout. I nodded. *It felt so good to see smoke and not be afraid,* she said. *That fog has come in the same way every evening for thousands of years.*

Yeah, I said, grateful.

Baby, let's get some dim sum, she said.

And then let's come back and make love.

The Smoke Week

NOTES

In this account, in the interest of privacy, I have changed the names of missing persons described in posters that appeared after September 11. Many thanks to Windows of Hope and to the National Geographic Society Afghan Girls Fund—both for the work they do and for letting me, through this book, be part of it—and to all the friends and family who gave me permission to use their names and quote their words.

While the National Geographic Society is aware of this work, *The Smoke Week* is neither associated with nor endorsed by the Society.

The New World: "THE BASTARDS!" was on the cover of the issue of *The Village Voice* that came out September 12, 2001.

The Cruelest Day: I borrow the idea of a God needing human hands to act from the end of Annie Dillard's book, *For the Time Being*. New York: Knopf, 1999.

"April is the cruelest month" is a line from "The Waste Land," by T. S. Eliot. *Collected Poems: 1909-1962*. New York: Harcourt Brace Jovanovich, 1936.

Every Broken Thing Made Whole: "By the waters of Babylon, we lay down and wept for thee, Zion" is from Psalms 137:1.

A Palliative: "The world of sports—a palliative for many Americans—was unavailable," comes from an article in *The New York Times* by Robert D. McFadden: "After the Attacks: an Overview; A Shaken Nation Struggles to Regain Its Equilibrium, but Remains on Edge." September 14, 2001. Copyright © 2001, *The New York Times*. Reprinted with permission.

Audre Lorde's words come from *The Cancer Journals*. Copyright © 1980 by Audre Lorde. Reprinted by permission of Aunt Lute Books.

Notes from the Week After: The line, "Over there is over here" comes from Suheir Hammad's poem, "first writing since." Copyright © 2001 by Suheir Hammad. Reprinted with permission.

A Few Words about the Bad Smell: I paraphrase information about the olfactory properties of violets from Diane Ackerman's *A Natural History of the Senses*. New York: Random House, 1990.

The definition of *acrid* is from *The New Shorter Oxford English Dictionary*, edited by Lesley Brown. Oxford University Press, 1993. Reprinted by permission of Oxford University Press.

The Friendly Skies: Richard Serra's account of seeing people "fall off those buildings like feathers" comes from an article in *The New York Times* by William L. Hamilton: "Neighbors, Shining Through: When the Nest Resists the Storm." September 20, 2001. Copyright © 2001, *The New York Times*. Reprinted with permission.

Books Available from Gival Press

A Change of Heart by David Garrett Izzo
    1st edition, ISBN 1-928589-18-9, $20.00

    A historical novel about Aldous Huxley and his circle "astonishingly alive and accurate."
    — Roger Lathbury, George Mason University

Barnyard Buddies I by Pamela Brown; illustrations by Annie H. Hutchins
    1st edition, ISBN 1-928589-15-4, $16.00

    Thirteen stories filled with a cast of creative creatures both engaging and educational. "These stories in this series are delightful. They are wise little fables, and I found them fabulous."
    — Robert Morgan, author of *This Rock* and *Gap Creek*

Barnyard Buddies II by Pamela Brown; illustrations by Annie H. Hutchins
    1st edition, ISBN 1-928589-21-9, $16.00

    "Children's literature which emphasizes good character development is a welcome addition to educators' as well as parents' resources."
    — Susan McCravy, elementary school teacher

Bones Washed With Wine: Flint Shards from Sussex and Bliss by Jeff Mann
    1st edition, ISBN 1-928589-14-6, $15.00

    A special collection of lyric intensity, including the 1999 Gival Press Poetry Award winning collection. Jeff Mann is "a poet to treasure both for the wealth of his language and the generosity of his spirit."
    — Edward Falco, author of *Acid*

Canciones para sola cuerda / Songs for a Single String by Jesús Gardea;
    English translation by Robert L. Giron
    1st edition, ISBN 1-928589-09-X, $15.00

    A moving collection of love poems, with echoes of *Neruda à la Mexicana* as Gardea writes about the primeval quest for the perfect woman. "The free verse...evokes the quality and forms of cante hondo, emphasizing the emotional interplay of human voice and guitar."
    — Elizabeth Huergo, Montgomery College

Dead Time / Tiempo muerto by Carlos Rubio
    1st edition, ISBN 1-928589-17-0, $21.00

    This bilingual (English/Spanish) novel is "an unusual tale of love, hate, passion and revenge."
    — Karen Sealy, author of *The Eighth House*

Dervish by Gerard Wozek
>1st edition, ISBN 1-928589-11-1, $15.00

>Winner of the 2000 Gival Press Poetry Award. This rich whirl of the dervish traverses a grand expanse from bars to crazy dreams to fruition of desire. "By Jove, these poems shimmer."
>— Gerry Gomez Pearlberg, author of *Mr. Bluebird*

Dreams and Other Ailments / Sueños y otros achaques by Teresa Bevin
>1st edition, ISBN 1-928589-13-8, $21.00

>Winner of the Bronze Award – 2001 *ForeWord Magazine*'s Book of the Year Award for Translation. A wonderful array of short stories about the fantasy of life and tragedy but filled with humor and hope. "*Dreams and Other Ailments* will lift your spirits."
>— Lynne Greeley, The University of Vermont

The Gay Herman Melville Reader by Ken Schellenberg
>1st edition, ISBN 1-928589-19-7, $16.00

>A superb selection of Melville's work. "Here in one anthology are the selections from which a serious argument can be made by both readers and scholars that a subtext exists that can be seen as homoerotic."
>— David Garrett Izzo, author of *Christopher Isherwood: His Era, His Gang, and the Legacy of the Truly Strong Man*

Let Orpheus Take Your Hand by George Klawitter
>1st edition, ISBN 1-928589-16-2, $15.00

>Winner of the 2001 Gival Press Poetry Award. A thought provoking work that mixes the spiritual with stealthy desire, with Orpheus leading us out of the pit. "These poems present deliciously sly metaphors of the erotic life that keep one reading on, and chuckling with pleasure."
>— Edward Field, author of *Stand Up, Friend, With Me*

Metamorphosis of the Serpent God by Robert L. Giron
>1st edition, ISBN 1-928589-07-3, $12.00

>"Robert Giron's biographical poetry embraces the past and the present, ethnic and sexual identity, themes both mythical and personal."
>— *The Midwest Book Review*

Middlebrow Annoyances: American Drama in the 21st Century by Myles Weber
>1st edition, ISBN 1-928589-20-0, $20.00

>"Weber's intelligence and integrity are unsurpassed by anyone writing about the American theatre today...."
>— John W. Crowley, The University of Alabama at Tuscaloosa

The Nature Sonnets by Jill Williams
1st edition, ISBN 1-928589-10-3, $8.95

An innovative collection of sonnets that speaks to the cycle of nature and life, crafted with wit and clarity. "Refreshing and pleasing."
— Miles David Moore, author of *The Bears of Paris*

The Smoke Week: Sept. 11-21, 2001 by Ellis Avery
1st edition, ISBN 1-928589-24-3, $15.00

Winner of the Ohioana Library Walter Rumsey Marvin Award
"Here is Witness. Here is Testimony."
— Maxine Hong Kingston, author of *The Fifth Book of Peace*

Songs for the Spirit by Robert L. Giron
1st edition, ISBN 1-928589-08-1, $16.95

This humanist psalter reflects a vision of the new millennium, one that speaks to readers regardless of their spiritual inclination. "This is an extraordinary book."
— John Shelby Spong, author of *Why Christianity Must Change or Die: A Bishop Speaks to Believers in Exile*

Tickets to a Closing Play by Janet I. Buck
1st edition, ISBN 1-928589-25-1, $15.00

Winner of the 2002 Gival Press Poetry Award
"...this rich and vibrant collection of poetry [is] not only serious and insightful, but a sheer delight to read."
— Jane Butkin Roth, editor, *We Used to Be Wives: Divorce Unveiled Through Poetry*

Wrestling with Wood by Robert L. Giron
3rd ed., ISBN 1-928589-05-7, $5.95

A chapbook of impressionist moods and feelings of a long-term relationship which ended in a tragic death. "Nuggets of truth and beauty sprout within our souls."
— Teresa Bevin, author of *Havana Split*

For Book Orders Only, Call: 800.247.6553
Or Write : Gival Press, LLC / PO Box 3812 / Arlington, VA 22203
Visit: www.givalpress.com

CPSIA information can be obtained
at www.ICGtesting.com
Printed in the USA
FSHW021323250122
87908FS